THE
RAILWAY JOURNEYS
OF MY
CHILDHOOD

To R.W.
with love
&
thanks to Bernard Kaukas

THE RAILWAY JOURNEYS · OF MY CHILDHOOD ·

BRIGADIER JOHN FAVIELL

PAN ORIGINAL
PAN BOOKS LONDON AND SYDNEY

FIRST PUBLISHED 1983 BY PAN BOOKS LTD,
CAVAYE PLACE, LONDON, SW10 9PG

© 1983 SHELDRAKE PRESS LTD
TEXT AND PICTURES © 1983 BRIGADIER JOHN FAVIELL

DESIGNED AND PRODUCED BY
SHELDRAKE PRESS LTD, 188 CAVENDISH ROAD,
LONDON, SW12 0DA

TYPESETTING BY: SX COMPOSING LTD
COLOUR ORIGINATION BY: LITHOSPEED LTD

ISBN 0 330 28179 8

PRINTED AND BOUND IN SPAIN
BY PRINTER INDUSTRIA GRAFICA,
BARCELONA.
DLB 10680 – 1983

JOHN FAVIELL was born in Blackheath in 1898. He had a distinguished military career that spanned both world wars. Following his education at Cheltenham College and the Royal Military Academy at Woolwich, he was commissioned into the Royal Field Artillery in 1916 and served on the Western Front, where he was wounded and mentioned in despatches.

After the war he spent some time in Ireland during the Troubles and then three years in India, followed by two years at the Staff College at Camberley. He was in Palestine during the Arab rebellion of 1936 where he was wounded and won the Military Cross. In the Second World War he served with the 9th Highland Division and later was appointed to a senior post at the War Office. He was awarded the O.B.E. in 1943, followed by the C.B.E. on his retirement in 1950. From 1951 to 1959 he was the Defence Adviser to the Conservative Research Department.

John Faviell married in 1942 the widow of Sir Alec Russell. She was the grand-daughter of Lord Russell of Killowen, and all the great grandchildren for whom this book was written derive from her first marriage: Edward, Andrew, Thomas, James, Dominic and Hugo. All the fabulous aunts and uncles, however, are on his side of the family: Aunt Edith (Royston, G.N.R.), Aunt Ines (Rampton, G.N.R.), Aunt Bee (Chiddingfold, L.S.W.R.) and Uncle Thorney (Kelsale, G.E.R.).

FOREWORD

By some happy chance, about four years ago a few charming water colour sketches of Edwardian railways, accompanied by equally delightful descriptions, fell on to my desk from the morning post. Manuscripts and drawings are always an interesting diversion in my job on the British Railways Board. Unknown to the author, these had been sent by one of his friends who felt they deserved a wider showing.

A meeting was soon arranged with Brigadier John Faviell in his sitting room at Great Maytham Hall in Kent, where he has chosen to spend his retirement. The scenario which then unfolded was better than any fictional creation. Brigadier Faviell had properly and wisely decided, as part of the testament of his busy and interesting life, to give to his grandchildren and their children a legacy of his childhood memories of the railways in their heyday of the Edwardian era. His remarkable visual recall of train journeys 80 years ago is matched by its factual accuracy; no mean feat when one considers that this was achieved without reference books. The fascination of steam railways which so entranced him is conveyed to us as though a window has been opened on the past; we see what he saw, feel what he felt.

The only role I claim for myself was to persuade him to share that happiness with countless other children from eight to 80 – that is, all of you. The golden myth of Edwardian England would appear to be true – at least as far as the unclouded happiness of that small boy was concerned.

Bernard Kaukas

CONTENTS

A NOTE ABOUT SOME COMMON TERMS,

In the series of illustrative memories that follow extreme accuracy has not been attempted and the expert may find some technical details missing. On the other hand expressions in common use throughout the age of steam may now mean little to some readers. After all, the steam age died quite a while ago. It may therefore be helpful to explain some of these terms – rapidly becoming old-fashioned – which occur from time to time. An attempt to do so follows.

CLASSIFICATION BY WHEEL ARRANGEMENT

Leading Wheels	Driving Wheels	Trailing Wheels	
2	2	2	} Single drivers
4	2	2	
4	4	0	"4 Coupler"
2	4	0	} Variations of 4 Coupled engines
0	4	2	
0	4	4	
4	4	2	'Atlantic'
4	6	0	"Six coupler"

BASIC FEATURES OF STEAM LOCOMOTIVES

4-4-0 Tender engine with outside cylinders

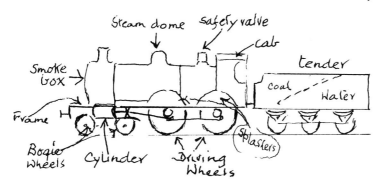

0-4-4 Tank engine with inside cylinders

This type could run equally well in either direction—a great asset in suburban services. Other types were the saddle tank with the water reservoir slung in a sort of saddle above the boiler and a pannier tank which had it slung lower, leaving the top of the boiler clear.

"Compound" means that the steam is used twice: after use in high-pressure cylinders it passes into those of low pressure. One set of cylinders is usually visible "outside" and the other invisible "inside."

INTRODUCTION

Many railway enthusiasts look back to the reign of King Edward as the heyday of steam. Be that as it may, those years still provide me with extraordinarily vivid memories, and it has not been difficult to recapture in words and pictures some of the rail journeys I made then.

One might say that steam and railways are in the Faviell blood. For generations Faviells have been railway engineers. My great grandfather, Mark Faviell, turned from canal building to railways in the very early days. There exist contracts of his and his brother's for the "Measuring and laying of rails" as early as 1835 and 1837 in the Birmingham and Manchester districts.

My grandfather, William F. Faviell, continued railway construction in a big way further afield. At the time the Indian Mutiny broke out he was building the line from Bombay up the precipitous Western Ghats towards Central India – a formidable task at that time. He, his wife and their three small children owed their lives to a faithful "Bearer" who warned them what was afoot in time for them to disappear into the jungle until the revolt quietened down. His next major task was the construction of the line from Kandy to Colombo in Ceylon, which he completed in 1864.

The fascination with steam certainly showed in my father, even though he became a marine engineer. My own generation went in different ways. Like so many at the opening of the 20th century most of us joined the armed services. Two of my cousins became Royal Engineers, two more became Indian Army officers and another was in the Royal Navy. I, the youngest, was commissioned into the Royal Field Artillery in 1916. But we kept alive the family's railway tradition with a continuing interest in everything to do with trains.

My interest must have been inbred. One of my very earliest recollections is of seeing a steamroller from the nursery window and being fascinated by its workings. Later when I registered railways I was even more fascinated. My father certainly fostered this involvement, but I suspect it was there before I was three.

John Faviell

Great Maytham Hall   March 1983

Chocolate & Cream of the GWR carriages. Here headed by
a Saddle Tank, a favourite of the G.W.R on coastal
routes such as this.

CHAPTER ONE

LONG, LONG AGO

At the turn of the century the thrill of a train journey for a small boy was as great as a trip by Concorde might be today.

For parents comparatively simple journeys in those days called for some organisation. Looking back it seems surprising how light-heartedly trips by train were undertaken and how complicated even the shorter ones would seem to us today.

My early childhood was spent in Blackheath, where we lived until I was ten, and my first train journeys occurred in and around London. When, for example, our mother thought a day in real country would be a good change for us from walks on the heath or in Greenwich Park, she took us to Hayes

Common (now much changed!). This was only some 12 miles away – nothing at all today, but then a considerable expedition. We were quite a party. There was Mother, Nanny, a seven-year-old boy, a girl of five and a boy not quite four (me) with our spaniel puppy Jim. Naturally too we had with us all the impedimenta of a picnic: a hamper, a rug, my sister's teddy; and my mother would have had her parasol.

This was our trip: first we took a horse tram to Lewisham, then by train (to my great delight) to Elmers End. There we changed and waited for the branch line train to Hayes Station. One memory of that day is absurdly clear: it was of the front view of the incredibly old engine that headed our train. At the

time its age was no consideration. Rather it was a curious feature, not seen before or since, which attracted the interest of a very small boy: a hollow space between the smoke box and the front buffers. Vaguely I see this engine as a 2-4-0 with outside frames and a plain topless windscreen type of cab.

It is clear to me now that this small branch line was run by completely antiquated engines and rolling stock. What I saw was probably an engine built as early as the 1860s. It would be understandable for an old warrior with more than 30 years of service to be put out to grass on a small branch line. Most likely it was one of the old Chatham and Dover locomotives built shortly before 1870 to take the Dover mails.

My misty recollection of the ancient 2-4-0 on the branch line from Elmers End to Hayes.

Changing at Elmers End, ready for the train to Hayes.

A typical first-class non-corridor c. 1901

CHAPTER TWO

A VISIT TO SOME LONDON TERMINI

G.N.R. "Big Atlantic".

The next great thrill in early days of the century was again when I was very small. My father, who realised that even then I was barmy on railways, organised a special trip for me in, I think, 1903, two years after King Edward VII came to the throne. I went up to his office in the City, deposited by my mother, I should imagine, because I was so very young. The plan was to tour some of the London termini. We took the old steam Metropolitan from the City to Euston. Then on to Kings Cross and St. Pancras stations.

At Euston I saw some interesting railway vans in what seemed a very dark station. Among the vans was what must have been a travelling Post Office car with its picking up nets and exchange apparatus discreetly folded away. This dropping and picking up of mails was an important part of the postal arrangements of the early 1900s. Along all the main lines at selected intervals were nets on posts each with a small hut from which the controller operated them. On the trains were Postal Carriages manned by G.P.O. sorters with a corridor "off central" in order to provide security from the rest of the train. The trains picked up and delivered these mails at speeds of up to 60 m.p.h., so the containers had to be very tough to withstand the heavy bump of the pick-up, and the net for catching them from the train was made of the strongest rope. The little hut was in communication with the nearest signal box which

Euston c. 1903

It seemed a dark low station but I saw some interesting luggage vans.

Mail exchanges at Speed

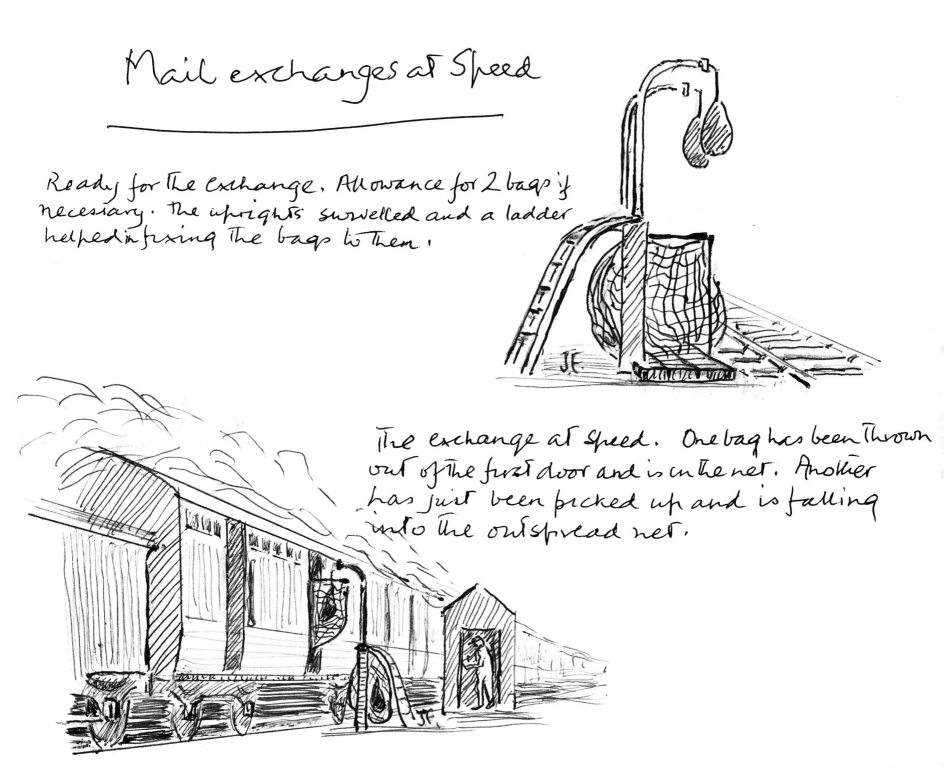

Ready for the exchange. Allowance for 2 bags if necessary. The uprights swivelled and a ladder helped in fixing the bags to them.

The exchange at speed. One bag has been thrown out of the first door and is in the net. Another has just been picked up and is falling into the outspread net.

17

Two Johnson singles at S? Pancras

warned the operator of the train's approach. It was a highly specialised job, particularly for the operator inside the car who had to know the exact position of each mail exchange point.

At Kings Cross was the first excitement – a brand new Atlantic of the Great Northern Railway – but the highlight of the whole tour came at St. Pancras. It was a fine day and we walked to the end of the main line departure platform and out into the sunlight beyond the roof of the station. There we found an express to Scotland headed by two of the charming Johnson Single Drivers. They had obviously been building up steam pressures for their start, and both their safety valves were at work with a loud noise and a stream of steam. The pilot engine was I remember beyond the end of the platform. Here they are as I remember them on that wonderful day so long ago.

At the end of Queen Victoria's

A glimpse of what I would have seen a few years later. One of the famous Midland Compounds about to handle the same express with ease.

reign the "Twopenny Tube" appeared. It was a good name for two reasons: first, the line was literally a continuous tube designed specifically for an electric train and in which a steam engine could not have run without asphyxiating its staff and passengers. Secondly, the charge was only 2d. for the whole or any section of the journey between the original two terminals of Shepherd's Bush and the Bank (part of what is now the Central Line).

It was not long before the old Metropolitan and District Railways – known to us simply as the Underground – electrified their systems. The advantages were certainly real as anyone who has travelled on the steam Underground will know. A treat for us children was an outing to the Earls Court exhibition in 1902, before electrification. After a drive in a "growler" (the old horse-drawn cab) from Blackheath down to New Cross,

we began our journey by the East London line with a change at Aldgate to the District for Earls Court. The carriages were filthy with the dirt and fumes of the smoky tunnels and also apparently flea-ridden. The result was that on return our Nanny adopted what became a standard drill: putting us straight into a bath so that we could be "de-flead". Whether the score of fleas found after these expeditions was ever satisfactory I cannot remember.

Edwardian enterprise.
One of the buses which provided a special service between the London termini of the main railway companies

The steam tank engines of the Metropolitan remained virtually unchanged from their first appearance in 1863 until electrification. A covered cab was the only noticeable improvement. Before we moved from Blackheath in 1908 electrification was complete. But as the Metropolitan and District were not built or designed for electric traction and small trains their new rolling stock differed markedly from that of the Twopenny Tube.

The old Metropolitan
a smoke outlet on the Inner circle

The old Metropolitan (basically what has since become known as the Circle Line) adopted carriages of essentially British design, rather similar to certain dining cars on the main lines except for curious iron concertina-type doors. The District on the other hand went all American with square-sided carriages. So it came about that in 1906 and for many years afterwards the Underground ran two contrasting types of rolling stock.

About this time another Tube was built; it was known as the Bakerloo Line because initially its terminals were at Baker Street and Waterloo. In construction and rolling stock, this line was similar to the Twopenny Tube. It began life by having lights all along the tunnel. There were glass doors at each end of the train and one could look goggle-eyed down the track. To young train enthusiasts such as me the views were fascinating, but obviously this expensive nonsense was soon stopped.

Heading the first "Twopenny Tube" train in 1900 was this rather cumbersome electric locomotive. Almost at once it was found unsuitable and replaced by multiple-unit trains.

About 1906. Metropolitan (left) and District (right) at their junction near Gloucester Road station

A Johnson Single at speed
with a Leeds express c. 1903

J.F.

CHAPTER THREE

TO BROADSTAIRS

ON THE S.E. & C.R.

The "curious cab" G.N.S.R. Transferred to S.E. & C.R.

On the viaducts. A "short set" suburban train on its way to Woolwich.

About the same time as my trip round London we all went down to Broadstairs on the South Eastern & Chatham Railway. We had a 3rd-class carriage of a very early vintage. The seats were of bamboo slats and the backs were short, so that one could look through the whole carriage. My father, who normally travelled 1st Class (this was probably typical of professional men of that period), was disgusted with this ancient carriage, but I was thrilled.

Nothing seemed to change on the S.E. & C.R. For nearly half a century they went on building short four-wheeled carriages for their suburban services, long after other vast suburban systems such as the London & South Western and the London Brighton & South Coast had launched out into bogie stock. These four-wheeled carriages produced rather uncomfortable rides: two heavy bumps, instead of the smoother rhythm of the bogies.

A main reason for this lack of progress was that the company, originally the South Eastern Railway, was too broke to build anything better. All south-east London was built up before the system was planned so, for some miles after spanning the Thames with two bridges, the lines had to be carried on continuous brick viaducts. These are still in use, a monument to the soundness of Victorian building, but the cost was terrific. Later the London Chatham & Dover was formed and

One of the last batch of engines built for the London Chatham & Dover, with new S.E. & C.R. lettering on the tender. A Kirtley 4-4-0 tidying up after taking water.

began to compete with the S.E.R.'s important cross-Channel traffic.

The S.E.R. wasted a great deal of money in futile quarrels with the L.C. & D., building extra lines and doubling up services in their efforts to win customers. But it was not until the Nineties that the logical action was taken and a combination effected under the name of the South Eastern & Chatham Railway. Long after 1900 both locomotives and rolling stock of L.C. & D. design were still to be seen on the S.E. & C.R. and I was always on the look-out for them.

At a station on our journey to Broadstairs we stopped opposite an engine with a most unusual cab which was entirely new to me. For many years I had no idea of the origin of this engine, nor, except on this journey to and from the Isle of Thanet (when I saw several), did I ever sight another of these curious cabs on the S.E. & C.R.

The mystery was accentuated when I first came in contact with the Great North of Scotland Railway more than 20 years later. There, in the far north of the British Isles, were what seemed to be engines identical to those I had seen in the extreme south-east corner of England. Certainly no one could mistake those curious cabs! The solution came later still. I discovered that these engines had first been built in the early Nineties for the G.N. of S. but that line could not afford to take delivery of the full order. The S.E. & C.R., who were

To Broadstairs in 1902 by S.E.C.R.
Father joins us from the City — 1st Class Comfort, with Loo!

The family returns. 3rd Class, hard seats, no Loo! JF

27

then rather short of motive power, bought five of the first batch. The ample cabs were no doubt designed as protection against the icy blasts of Aberdeenshire but they would have been a nice change in east Kent from the inadequate cabs of the old S.E. & C.R.

On our early journeys from Lewisham to Charing Cross my brother and I soon established a series of "look-outs" – places where items of special interest could be spotted. He was four years my senior so I merely followed his greater knowledge.

On joining the main line at St. Johns we peered upwards at a small spur from Nunhead which crossed over our line near that station. Standing on the bridge above us there was usually an old 0-4-2 Tank of London Chatham & Dover design.

At New Cross we looked right and with luck a Metropolitan train would show itself on the line from Whitechapel. For the first few years it would have been headed by one of the 4-4-0 Metro Tanks; later it would have been the first version of their electric trains.

Approaching Spa Road Station, long since abandoned, we looked right again across Bermondsey for a glimpse of Tower Bridge and the masts of the many steamers then loading and unloading in the Pool of London.

Finally, to our left, there were the London Brighton & South Coast Railway metals which ran parallel with ours into London Bridge. This, the last of our look-outs, held the greatest hopes. We would be virtually certain of seeing some beautiful bright yellow engine. When D. E. Marsh produced his Brighton Atlantics we hoped to see one but we never did. However, a little Stroudley 0-4-2 Tank and the famous Gladstone 0-4-2 Tender engines were often to be seen. Whatever we saw, the L.B. & S.C.R. engines provided a fitting finale to our trip.

Apart from our special look-out

Our first Look-out. ex L.C & D.R. 0-4-2 Tank above was, we reach St Johns Station

Our final look out – A "Gladstone" backing out of London Bridge

places we always kept an eye open for any engines of the S. E. & C.R. main-line trains which might pass us after St. Johns Station, Lewisham. Our ambition was to see one of the handsome 4-4-0s recently built by H. S. Wainright for the main-line expresses. But all we ever saw were the old Stirling engines built many years earlier.

After our move from Blackheath in 1908 I became a boarder at prep school, Shirley House, Old Charlton in Kent, and once more came into contact with these old Stirling engines. My journey home for the holidays began at Charlton Station. With other little boys bound for London and beyond we walked out of school skirting the walls of Charlton Park, then in its original untouched state, and passed St. John's Church where I had the terrifying ordeal of singing solos in the choir. At the station a fairly long wait for our stopping train to London was usual and often a fast train from Dartford would pass through first. When this happened it was always headed by a Stirling 4-4-0 in its original condition of about 1890.

Our train deposited me at what was then called Waterloo Junction, S. E. & C.R. I walked up the passage to the Waterloo terminus of the L.S.W.R. beside which a single line then ran

1908

The express from Dartford sails
through Charlton as we wait for
our stopping train. It is headed
by an old Stirling 4-4-0 in
original condition

connecting the two railway systems. Generally there was the odd luggage van on this line waiting to be shunted and sometimes a tank engine ready to perform that task.

Years later, in 1916, I met the Stirling engines again. Then I was at the "shop" – The Royal Military Academy, Woolwich. When we had a weekend we used to take a Saturday midday train from Woolwich Arsenal to London. This was in fact the same fast train from Dartford I used to see at Charlton – non-stop from Woolwich Arsenal to London Bridge. It was still drawn by a Stirling 4-4-0! But by this time the old engine had had a slight renovation: a more modern cab and a steam dome instead of the old dual purpose safety valve. Otherwise it was much as originally built nearly 30 years earlier.

The S.E.C.R. went in for "bird cage lookouts" on their brake vans, on main line trains as well as suburban. This example of the latter is headed (first built in the 1880's) by a Stirling 0-4-4 Tank. They were still going strong when we left Blackheath in 1908.

The Continental Boat Train c 1906. A Wainwright "D" 4-4-0 in command

CHAPTER·FOUR

TO BATH ON THE G.W.R.

Early in 1904 my father was recovering from rheumatic fever and decided to spend some weeks in Bath for a cure in the spa waters. The whole family was to go with him, and it would be my first trip on a Great Western Railway main-line train with the glamour of departure from the express platform at Paddington.

To my young eyes the vast roof of Paddington Station was impressive, but I was sorry not to see the engine heading our train. We were a large family party, complete with Nanny and the mountains of luggage felt necessary for a long stay away from home in those days. Finding our seats (booked ahead) and checking the storage of belongings left no time for wanderings up the platform. However I found compensation in the carriages. The train was made up of complete corridor stock, each coach with a side passage or corridor from which sliding doors led into the separate compartments. The roofs were the clerestory, square-ended type developed so early by the G.W.R. All new to me and thrilling.

But more was to come. Towards the end of the journey I was standing in the corridor when the engine whistle sounded shrilly. Shouts of "come in and shut the door". I was hardly inside when we roared into the blackness of a tunnel. Near the village of Box this tunnel took the line deep under the Wiltshire hills to

32

the Avon Valley and Bath. It was the famous Box Tunnel built by Brunel; when completed in 1841 it was, at 1¾ miles, the longest railway tunnel in the world. On one of our trips from Bath we were able to see the western entrance. Typical of Brunel's stylish finishes, this was a magnificent classical structure.

For the last few weeks of our stay at Bath my father took the daily breakfast car express from Bath to Paddington, stopping only at Swindon; he came back in the evening after I was in bed. As a small boy I always went down to Bath station to see him leave for this formidable commuting trip. G.W.R. Single Drivers still headed this train, and climbing out of Bath these fine engines always skidded on starting. My memory of this sound is still clear.

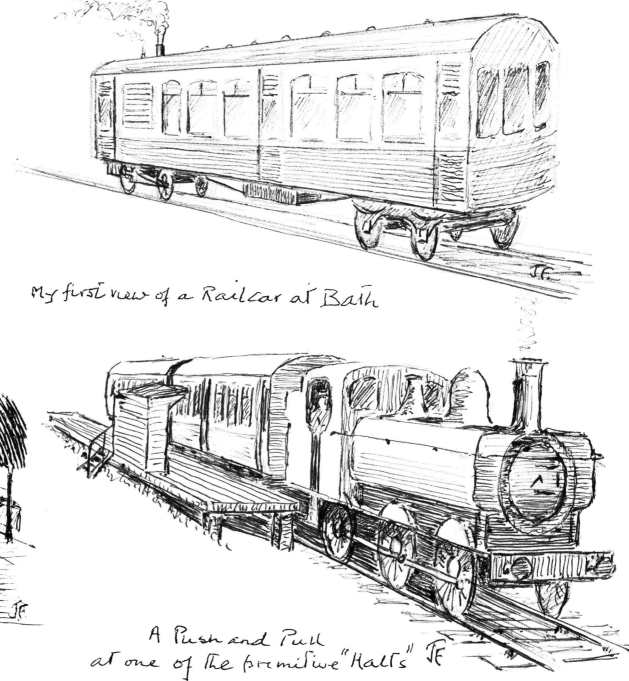

My first view of a Railcar at Bath

Paddington c. 1904

A Push and Pull at one of the primitive "Halls" JE

33

Another new sight at Bath station was the City class 4-4-0, the first of the long line of engines with tapered boilers introduced in this country by the G.W.R. Appropriately, the first I saw was *City of Bath*. But I also saw *City of Truro* and later learnt that she was the first locomotive to reach an authenticated speed of more than 100 m.p.h., in 1904.

Our rooms in Bath were not far from the station and from them a glimpse of the lines approaching it could be seen. The location therefore suited me admirably; but now I wonder how my parents found it. The house was owned by an Austrian couple who spoke excellent English and were charming. Clearly they must have returned to Austria soon after the end of our stay because we had letters from them for many months afterwards with Austrian stamps. These we children seized with relish for our stamp collection. Perhaps the couple remembered our collections because each letter seemed to have stamps of different denominations; if this was so I hope their thoughtfulness was · acknowledged by someone.

One morning I had another first view, this time of a "Rail Motor" or "Rail Car" as it was popularly called; locally it was known just as "the Car". At this period several of the main companies experimented with these cars for short branch lines where traffic was light. The early efforts, pressed forward

The Race from the West
G.W.R. "Duke of Connaught" on the record run of 1904 with the "Mails special".

A London express emerging from 'Box Tunnel'
c. 1904.

by the G.W.R., resulted in a single coach with a tiny built-in engine at one end and the funnel sticking up out of the carriage roof. It was this version that I saw.

A great advantage in the rail car plan was that a full-sized station was unnecessary; a short platform and a small hut as shelter were sufficient. These simple stopping places were called halts and a few remain even today.

The idea of rail cars was eminently sound and economical but these tiny engines proved temperamental and were gradually replaced by Tank engines permanently attached to one or two normal carriages and capable of being run in either direction without turning the engine round. These later versions continued in use for many years and were known as "push & pulls".

Some steam "push & pulls" were still running well into the days of British Railways. The example shown has an ex-G.W.R. 0-6-0 pannier tank engine. The two carriages were specially built for the outfit with the controls passing through them from the engine to the end of the second carriage, in which there was a driver's compartment for use when the engine pushed rather than pulled. One of the more primitive halts has been illustrated. No ticket office, just a short platform and a tiny shelter. Tickets were issued on the train as indeed they are on some branch lines today where the Diesel equivalent of the steam rail car operates.

In 1912 I had my first journey in a rail car. I had just joined the Natural History Society of Cheltenham College, which was very popular because it let us have an occasional outing and provided welcome relief from our monastic existence. One such outing to the Forest of Dean involved a complicated rail journey with changes at Gloucester and (I think) Newnham. The last stage of our journey was by rail car. There were two carriages with the tiny engine inside the first. I remember being impressed with the acceleration on starting, but the forest was so lovely it overshadowed other memories, even of the trains!

One of Brunel's many Triumphs; The Royal Albert Bridge over the Tamar from Saltash. As in C. 1904.

CHAPTER FIVE

ROYSTON, THE G.N.R.

Our train to Royston, the big
clerestory coach in the middle.

AND A LIFELIKE
MODEL RAILWAY

Still going strong, an "Eight footer" leading
a G.N.R. express in 1903 (originally built in 1870)

I made my first acquaintance with the Great Northern Railway in May or June, 1905, when we went to stay with an aunt and uncle at Royston.

As usual we formed a considerable party with a lot of luggage. We left from Lewisham Junction, the nearest station to our house. Unless we took a train late in the morning, a change at London Bridge was necessary for Charing Cross. On this trip the change was the first obstacle and demanded careful marshalling of us children and our clobber. Then across London from Charing Cross to Kings Cross. We were more than one "growler" could carry; indeed two only just did it and they had to be kept together. All this would no doubt have worked without too much fuss had it not been for a hold-up on nearing Kings Cross. We learned from our cabby that the departure of King Edward VII on a journey to the north was causing the delay. Policemen were everywhere and nothing moved. We sat helpless in our cab, Mother fussing, children fidgeting, while a string of cabbies ahead and behind us shouted their feelings to one another and to the world in general.

We moved at last, just in time to hurl ourselves and belongings into the train for Royston, while our porter literally threw our trunks into the guard's van. This eventful beginning added to the excitement of travelling on the G.N.R. I had been told we would be on the main line as far as Hitchin, our first stop. This was one of the lines over which the "Race to the North" was run 10 years or so earlier.

After the opening of through routes from London to Edinburgh and Aberdeen, keen competition had developed between the west coast route to Scotland, operated by the London and North Western Railway as far as Carlisle and the Caledonian Railway

Leaving Peterborough for the Norfolk coast Midland & Great Northern Joint, with a Train of old G.N.R. carriages. c. 1905.

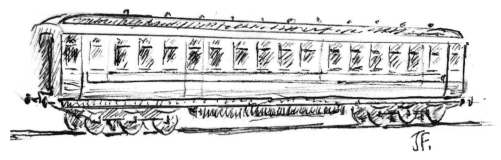

An early G.N.R. Dining Car

beyond, and the east coast route operated jointly by the Great Northern and North Eastern Railways. The race which became famous was in 1895. The L.N.W.R. made the fastest time, covering the 141.2 miles from Crewe to Carlisle at an *average* of 67 m.p.h. The hero of this record-breaking performance was an engine called *Hardwicke*.

Our train to Royston consisted of an old 2-4-0 pulling four or five old non-corridor six-wheelers and one much more modern clerestory corridor coach; to my delight my parents selected the latter. I told my father that our carriage had six-wheel bogies and I remember really thinking I had seen these. He said nonsense, there were no six-wheel bogies, except on sleeping cars and a few dining cars. But I still seem to remember those six-wheeled bogies. Perhaps it was an old converted diner? Anyway I have shown them in my sketch of the train to Royston.

Unfortunately I disgraced myself both on the journey and on arrival at Royston. I had secretly brought with me two woolly bear caterpillars in a matchbox. When taken out from my pocket for air they escaped and crawled towards female passengers sitting next to me; their consternation was great and so was the ticking-off I had from my mother!

Then I began to sneeze and sneeze and feel rather hot and queasy. The other passengers squashed themselves as far away as was possible. At Royston my uncle, who had been an R.A.M.C. Colonel, examined me. There on my chest a tell-tale rash was beginning to show – measles!

There was much to see at my uncle and aunt's. My cousins who were older than me and away at school had built a model railway in the paddock and I longed to see it. But the measles hit me badly and I was many days in bed. For my mother it must have been a nuisance because I had to be left behind while she returned with my elder sister to start her off at school. Fortunately, our Nanny always came with us on these trips so

my mother would have had no anxiety about me. Indeed with Nanny acting as nurse under the supervision of a retired Colonel R.A.M.C. I could not have been in better hands.

Of all the summers of my childhood that one of 1905 alone I associate with rain. The time came when I was up but allowed out *only* if it was fine. For an age it seemed the rain would never stop. Each day I was told, "Don't worry, dear, it will be fine tomorrow". The feeling of frustration is still clear and I have no doubt it must have made me fractious and tiresome. There was so much to see outside: a vast garden (and I was beginning to get interested in birds) and the paddock with the model railway. At last the rain stopped and I was allowed into the garden and shown what my aunt said was a flycatcher's nest in a currant bush. Now that I know about birds and their nests it is clear that it certainly was not a flycatcher – more likely a blackcap.

Then came what I had seen in my dreams for ages – the model railway. It was a wonderful layout with realistic cuttings, embankments and tunnels. I only regretted the absence of engines and trains, which my cousins kept locked up when they were away. My own efforts were confined to a simple layout on the attic floor of our Blackheath house. Cuttings and embankments were impossible and although I was given a tunnel it looked absurdly unrealistic on the bare floorboards. Moreover, my gauge was the smallest, o. My cousins' gauge was 1, and this meant that standard drainpipes were just the right size for their tunnels. Carefully selected shingle

could also pass quite easily for ballast under their larger lines and children's bricks proved useful in bridging works over imaginary streams.

We had another journey on the G.N.R. the following Christmas. There was a great family gathering at the spacious house of another aunt and uncle near Retford. We were well supplied with aunts and uncles, which was not surprising because my father was one of nine and my mother of seven. This aunt and uncle were rather grand and then owned Rampton Manor, since converted into a well known lunatic asylum – or perhaps what should now

be called a mental hospital. Our train to Retford was an express to the north stopping only at Peterborough and that stop proved to be the highlight of the journey. On another platform directly level with our carriage stood a small bright yellow 4-4-0 engine. It was a Midland & Great Northern Joint locomotive and a rare sight indeed; it was heading a train of old G.N.R. carriages. As we watched the whistle sounded, the guard's flag waved and the train prepared to move off – no doubt bound for the Norfolk coast. These little engines, which were well balanced and attractive, came from the Midland

Our journey to Retford
G.N.R "Big Atlantic"   c.1905

works at Derby. They remained the mainstay of the Midland & Great Northern Joint for many years. Like so many 4-4-0s built by S. W. Johnson for the Midland, some of these M. & G.N.J. engines were rebuilt and ran on into venerable old age.

There were some memorable occasions during this Christmas gathering. Rampton Manor was a vast house even for those spacious days and I was a very small boy. Early one morning I escaped from the eagle eyes of the grown-ups and set off to explore the first floor. Naturally I lost my way and, opening a door near the end of a passage, I toddled into a surprising scene. There was my aunt, naked and beginning to put on her "combs" – combinations are a virtually unknown garment today, but were useful before central heating became general! I froze with horror, then managed to creep away without being spotted. But the unexpected picture remained in my memory.

The final event of our stay was the Boxing Day Meet of the local foxhounds at the house. There was a light covering of snow but the day was sunny and crisp. We all assembled to greet the riders and for the grown-ups there were stirrup cups in profusion. For me it was the first experience of Huntsmen and Hounds and the Field arriving. Pink coats galore and the ladies all riding side saddle. Little did I think that one day I would ride to hounds myself. That was many years later when side saddles and pink coats were rarer as also were great houses with their supply of stirrup cups.

I dream of working the model railway JF.

CHAPTER SIX

ABOUT EXPRESS ENGINES

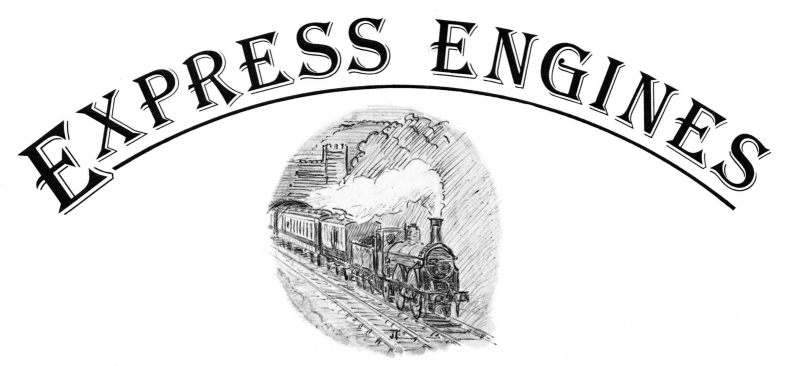

AND ROLLING STOCK OF THE PERIOD

EXPRESS LOCOMOTIVES

When King Edward came to the throne many of the main line expresses were still headed by Single Drivers, notably on the Midland and the Great Western. But after continuous and outstanding performance in the later years of Victoria's reign, they were beginning to be replaced by more powerful engines of 4-4-0 wheel arrangement. In the four years between 1900 and 1904 a vast range of this type of engine was produced by every major line in the United Kingdom. This period therefore might well be called the age of the 4-4-0. Among the more outstanding of these engines were the Midland Compounds, the Claud Hamiltons of the G.E.R., the Precursors of the L.N.W.R., the G.W.R. Cities and the bigger version of the Caledonian's Dunalastairs. The Midland Compounds were so successful that they were even continued by British Railways over 40 years later; all the other engines I have mentioned continued in service with only slight improvements for nearly as long.

It seems that Britain fell in love with the 4-4-0 for a much longer time than any other nation. So much so that all sorts of rebuilds and renovations of engines of this wheel arrangement took place. For example, the G.W.R. had produced a good-looking series called the Dukes followed by the blunt and solid Bulldogs. Some years later the frames and wheels of one were welded to the boilers of the other resulting in the Duke Dogs. These engines did valiant work on the Cambrian Railways' Welsh lines, which the G.W.R. took over after the original grouping following the first war, and on many other minor lines of

A Duke Dog in Wales on the Cambrian Lines
as it appeared many years later

that country for years after.

In my youngest train-watcher days the 4-4-0 was clearly the norm.

ATLANTICS AND SIX COUPLERS

As early as 1904 engine builders were on the threshold of other developments. The increased weight of trains had brought a search for greater tractive effort. The improvement took two forms of wheel arrangement under a bigger boiler with a bigger heating surface. Some systems went for the 4-6-0 – the Six Coupler; others developed the 4-4-2 – the Atlantic. Still others

switched from one to the other.

Strangely enough the first Six-Coupler was produced not by one of the great companies serving the industrial areas of Britain, but by the Highland Railway which covered the far north of the British Isles. This engine was built way back in 1894 and created something of a sensation at the time, not only on account of its new wheel arrangement but also because of its great size. Designed by David Jones, primarily for goods traffic, it became known as the "Jones Goods". It was an extremely satisfactory engine and led later to the

Castle class which proved an even greater success for the Highland's passenger service.

As a boy I watched all these developments with enthusiasm. I looked for big boilers and short funnels which were the most noticeable features of the new generation of locomotives. I had an older relative in Rugby who was studying to be an engineer and he sent me a mass of postcards of all the L.N.W.R. engines soon after they were first photographed, but in one of our moves my collection was thrown away. What I would give to have it back!

The L.N.W.R "Precursor" was a very successful design, capable of hauling the express trains which had previously necessitated double heading on the more difficult routes.

45

A famous six-coupler on the Cornish coast.
A G.W.R. 4-6-0 of the "Star" class. Designed
by Churchward This was a great step forward in
Locomotive construction and the basis of future express
engines of the G.W.R.

The "Caley". Pounding up Beatock.
A Dunalastair heading a
Perth express c. 1903

J.F.

47

TAKING ON WATER

One notable improvement during this period in the performance of long distance express traffic was the water trough. Initially the length of a non-stop journey was limited by the need to refill with water and this was a time consuming process. Moreover as speeds increased and trains became heavier either refills of water had to be more frequent or tenders increased in size so as to provide greater capacity for water.

The answer was the water trough between the rails, from which water could be scooped up at speed by a special attachment fitted under the tender. These troughs were sited at appropriate places on most of the main systems where trains would be travelling at speed. Naturally a mass of spray would shoot out as the water was scooped up and I well remember how drenched I got when putting my head out of the window to watch this operation for the

first time in about 1906.

The L.S.W.R. never adopted the system for their West Country expresses. Instead they began to build vast tenders carried on bogies. But when their successors, the Southern Railway, instituted the *Devon Belle* with its first stop at Exeter, they were in trouble. Even with enlarged tenders there would not be sufficient water to last over that distance. Rather than stop to refill they made an unofficial stop at Wilton and

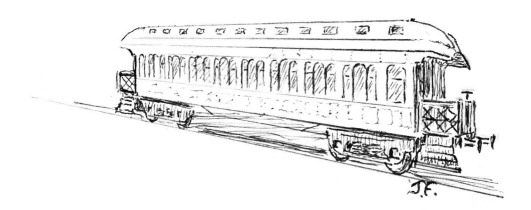

The first day Pullman to run on British rails.
Imported from America by the Midland Railway
and soon followed by a "Sleeper" pullman
for the same railway.

Probably the first of the fully composite bogie carriages.
Built about 1875 for the G.W.R Broad gauge.

EXPRESS ROLLING STOCK
Throughout Edwardian days it was possible to recognise any train on a main line by its colour and shape. Each railway company had a distinctive livery and developed its own particular design changed engines with extraordinary speed. This of course was over a quarter of a century later but I was lucky to be on the train to watch this performance.

For example the Midland favoured a deep red for both engines and rolling stock. The G.N.R. and the G.W.R. both had green engines, but the former had varnished teak carriages while the latter had the famous chocolate and cream. The L.N.W.R. engines were black, L.B. & S.C.R. had gamboge (bright deep yellow) engines, the for the windows and roofs of its rolling stock.

Caledonian and the G.E.R. blue. So there were endless combinations of colour, each peculiar to one railway.

The period we are considering could be called the age of the clerestory roof. Two distinct types of clerestory developed, one square-ended and the other curved. The square-ended was pioneered by the G.W.R., which produced a forward-looking carriage of this sort way back in the early 1890s, and

On the Troughs. A Midland compound of 1908 picking up water at speed.

J.F.

The old fashioned way.
A GER 2-4-0 taking
water from the station pipe c.1902

J.E.

Examples of the differing "styling" of carriages

Apart from the striking differences in colour adopted by each of the old Railway Companies there were marked contrasts in form in their outward appearance, particularly in the shape of windows

Simple and square. L.N.W.R.

everything rounded S.E.&C.R.
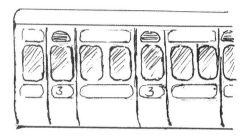

elegant and intricate G.N.R.
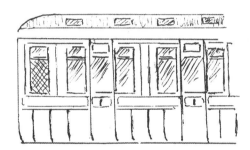

A pleasant compromise G.E.R.
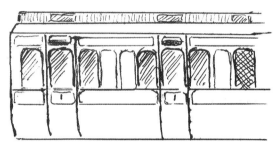

adopted wholeheartedly by the Midland, the North Eastern and the G.E.R. The G.N.R. persisted in the curved-end type introduced even earlier from America; and the American-style Pullmans included in many of the expresses of the Brighton and the S.E. & C.R. were also curved-ended. The L.N.W.R. was alone among the great English railway systems in retaining a flattish roof for their corridor stock, but all their sleeping and restaurant cars were curved-end clerestories with six-wheeled bogies.

Shapes of doors and windows were also individual. The L.N.W.R. adopted rather low square-cornered windows. The Midland on the other hand took to deep windows with attractive little lights above them. The main systems of the south, particularly the L.S.W.R. and the S.E. & C.R., went for roundness – round-cornered windows and round roofs.

The American influence on rolling stock began in the late 1870s when the Midland imported a sleeper from the United States. The interior as well as exterior provided novel features. There were six longitudinal bunks, with curtains, in an open saloon, a plan which was already usual in America; but also five separate compartments called "state rooms" from which arrangement the British sleeper clearly derived. This was a significant step and one typical of the enterprise of the Midland Railway.

The importation of American coaches was the first step towards introducing what became known as Pullmans. The name of course derived from the Pullman Company of America

Fitting in Lavatories

Early types of carriages for express trains

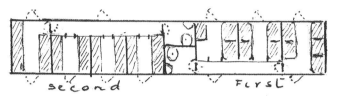

Semi corridor carriage. 3 first class
(c. 1900) 4 second with central lavatory for each section

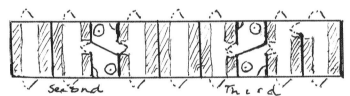

Non-corridor carriage. 3 second class, 4 thirds.
(c 1903) 5 of the compartments connected to the two sets of lavatories. Used on the Dover boat trains at that time

and gradually more and more British companies took to what appeared then as spectacular coaches. After causing some suspicion at first, they had a marked influence both on the design of our own carriages and the comfort of our trains. At the time their size and luxury were indeed unrivalled.

At first one or two Pullman coaches were introduced as part of express trains with an extra charge for the privilege of travelling in them. Gradually complete Pullman trains appeared with special names which soon became famous, such as the *Southern Belle*, later the *Brighton Belle*. For many years the distinctive look of the Pullman car with its curved-end clerestory roof remained unaltered. The early versions had six-wheeled bogies and above the windows was the word "Pullman" in gold letters. Each car had its own name in a scroll below the windows, such as the *Grosvenor*, the *Princess Helen*, the *Duchess of Norfolk*, the *Belgravia* and so on. Even the interior decoration, always sumptuous, was designed to fit the name. The *Grosvenor* was in the Adam style: mahogany, satinwood and green morocco upholstery. The *Princess Helen* had purple kingwood framing its bright mahogany and its deep chairs were drab striped moquette over a green background. Renaissance features were embodied when the name had classical connections.

The advent of lavatory facilities and dining cars produced a variety of different layouts in both carriages and trains. Even on main line trains known as "semi-fast" one could come across all sorts of carriages. Old stock was still in

There were still some hand operated turntables
to be seen; considering the weight of an express
engine it was a remarkably simple operation.
This is a "Precursor" of the L & N.W.R. being turned

use as new models came along, and the latter included some experiments in fitting lavatories and corridors. Then there were the composite carriages including two or even three classes of compartments, a lavatory and a tiny guard's van for luggage. For a time this type was much used on the L.N.W.R., which went in for detaching single coaches at junctions serving branch lines, though they did sometimes slip composite carriages at Blisworth, Rugby, Nuneaton and elsewhere, following the practice so popular on other systems such as the G.W.R. and G.E.R.

Many schemes for the fitting in of lavatories were adopted in the early days. Before the general use of corridor trains there were two major developments. The first, which remained the standard for the S.E. & C.R. for many years, was to have the lavatory in between two 1st-class compartments and, when this luxury was extended beyond 1st class, to have one side of the lavatory compartment connected with two or three 3rd-class compartments by a corridor.

The object was to reduce as little as possible the seating capacity of the carriage and to this end some systems introduced what became known as the semi-corridor, a type of coach which I first met on the G.E.R. By the end of the Edwardian era we had begun to reach, at least for long distance travel, the side corridor coach with the lavatory neatly tucked away at its ends.

Passengers both rich and poor had a large amount of comfort and convenience in these old-fashioned days. Porters were plentiful for both 1st- or 3rd-class passengers (2nd-class accommodation was then being phased out on most lines to provide more room for the overcrowded 3rd class); there was no difficulty in having luggage of any size or weight carried to carriage or luggage van. There was no incomprehensible loudspeaker voice giving out departures, arrivals or changes which the keenest ear could hardly decipher; instead there were plenty of good solid men about every station willing to answer any question in good solid old-fashioned but eminently

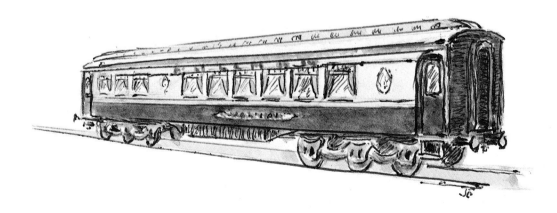

An early Pullman for the L.B.& S.C.R. Southern Belle

Kitchen of a restaurant
car G.E.R. c. 1908

Originally every Pullman car
had its own trained attendants
in this distinctive dress, with the
word Pullman on their lapels.

polite language. Their intimate knowledge of everything to do with "their" railway was equal to that of their locality. The man on the railway whether signalman, porter, ticket issuer or goods clerk was generally a man of the locality.

One did not have to be very rich to benefit from all sorts of what would now be considered as inordinate luxuries. The dining cars which were appearing on most of the long distance expresses provided simple but good meals served by proficient waiters at low costs. All the early dining cars were divided into two parts, the 1st class being separated from the rest by a passage and generally having a rather more roomy seating plan. But in other respects there was no real difference. The menu and the efficient service were the same. If preferred it was still possible to order a hamper lunch of cold chicken and salad at most of the main stations, the hamper being left for collection at a later stop. This was a relic of the days before dining cars. At certain stations local specialities were available on the platform. I remember that we always bought Banbury cakes at Banbury.

There were also special carriages like invalid saloons and family saloons which could be ordered provided a certain number of tickets were purchased. They were tacked on to any train and so relieved the passengers of the bother of changes. One could travel from let us say Bournemouth to Newcastle in the same carriage although passing over three different railway systems and probably attached to four different trains. The saloons were fully equipped with everything needed for a long journey. This mode of travel is a forgotten luxury indeed.

THE MAIN LINES,
THEIR LOCOMOTIVES
AND LIVERIES
L.N.W.R.

In 1903 a change took place in the direction of locomotive building on the L.N.W.R. The engineer F.W. Webb retired and was succeeded by George Whale. Under him the company went in for simpler express locomotives which proved to be much more reliable in service. The year after Whale took over, the first of the L.N.W.R. Precursor 4-4-0s appeared. They proved winners, and from them were developed the Experiment class and later the famous superheated George V 4-4-0s and the Prince of Wales 4-6-0.

The carriages of this "Premier Line" were not so great. The pure black and white colouring was attractive, but interior comfort was poor. Roofs were low and foot space cramped. The sleeping cars built for the west coast route to Scotland were a different matter – luxurious and smooth running.

East Coast Joint stock, Corridor Coach
1900 to 1909. handsome body work

West Coast Joint stock Corridor
1900 to 1909.

L.N.W.R "Precursor"

The Midland Red. Square ended
clerestory stock headed by rebuilt Johnson 4—4—0

A "Family Saloon" of about 1904

MIDLAND

In many ways the Midland was an intriguing railway. A number of famous, but what one might call lightweight engines came from their works at Derby and their coaches were supreme. Also they were unique in having a uniform deep rose madder colour for both engines and carriages.

The Midland Compound was one of their star performers. Produced by J. W. Johnson in 1902 and modified and improved by R. M. Deeley in about 1905, it was the mainstay of the Midland for some 20 years. And after superheating and further modification it was a standard London Midland Scottish express locomotive for the northern section for many years more.

The Edwardian Midland carriages were the tops in comfort and looks. Their clerestory roofs had blunt ends – unlike those of G.N.R. The deep twin-pane windows gave the maximum light, and leg room was exceptionally generous. Even the Midland branch lines had most comfortable coaches with these beautiful clerestory roofs.

I experienced this style of travel as late as 1917. When recovering in Leicester General Hospital from a war wound I often did the short railway journey to Melton Mowbray where an aunt lived. On this very short trip the comfort of the Midland non-corridor coaches was outstanding.

G.W.R.

I was not the only one of my generation to extol the Great Western Railway. To many of us their locomotives seemed supreme. Just as the Midland set the pace in rolling stock design so the G.W.R. produced innovations in the design of locomotives, of which several ultimately became standard practice. One such was the tapered boiler which proved to be a revolution in steam production and conservation. Another was the uplifted frame which provided accessibility for connecting rods and other working parts and simplified the layout of the frame as a whole.

In 1907 G. J. Churchward produced the Star class for the G.W.R. which embodied these and other new features. This class was so successful that it formed the basis of all future construction of express locomotives at Swindon until the end of the steam era, culminating in the King class.

G.N.R.

The G.N.R. produced a sensational engine in the first "Big Atlantic" Ivatt's in 1902. (H. A. Ivatt was the builder of a number of G.N.R locomotives, each known as Ivatt's.) With modifications by Sir Nigel Gresley, these engines did marvellous work on the east coast route for some 20 years.

I always thought early Edwardian corridor coaches of the east coast route preferable to those of the west. For one thing their clerestory roofs gave them a very attractive appearance with more head room and light for the passenger and for another the teak coloured coaches combined well with the apple green of the engine.

N.E.R. } Old type boiler and
Atlantic} main frame

G.W.R } New tapered boiler
surrounded and uplifted frame

G.N.R. Ivatt's "Big Atlantic.

A Midland "Compound"

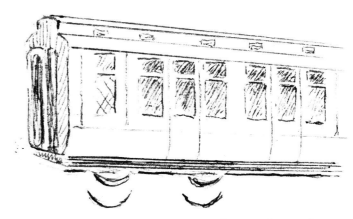

Midland Corridor coach 1901 to 1911.

A Midland Pullman Sleeper c. 1890.

CHAPTER SEVEN

KELSALE PLACE

Slowing to stop at Saxmundham,
An early oil fired Claud Hamilton

AND THE G.E.R.

Our arrival at Saxmundham station; heading
the train was a brand new Claud Hamilton. It was
an express to Yarmouth. Uncle Thorney greets us all.
The branch train to Aldeburgh waits in the distance

Edwardian Elegance
A typical dining car of the period,
flowers on the table and many minions!

Among our many aunts and uncles was a couple who lived at Kelsale Place, a few miles north of Saxmundham in Suffolk. They had no children of their own and seemed to like us little horrors being brought down to stay almost every summer holiday for year after year until shortly before the First World War. Our uncle, John Thornton King, known to us as Uncle Thorney, was easily our favourite and Kelsale Place was also our favourite place for visits. It provided us with many opportunities to travel on the Great Eastern Railway. The line from Liverpool Street served Yarmouth as well as Lowestoft. Except for one express, all the Yarmouth trains stopped at Saxmundham where we alighted and connected thence with the branch line to Leiston and Aldeburgh, so we were well provided for. We used to take a mid-morning express which stopped only at Ipswich before Saxmundham, and a similar early afternoon train on our return at the end of the holidays. In the up direction there was even one express from Lowestoft which ran non-stop from Saxmundham to Liverpool Street.

On our first trip in about 1903 we arrived in good time at Liverpool Street for our G.E.R. train. No doubt my eyes were popping out like prawns at all the unaccustomed sights, but one memory stands out. My father must have persuaded the driver of our train's engine – one of the then brand new Claud Hamiltons – to allow us into his cab. I was handed up to see all the beautiful shiny levers and shown by the stoker his great stack of coal. The next unforgettable picture of that trip is of the fields, trees and hedges of Suffolk looking marvellous to me after the dullness of Blackheath – particularly as I was seeing all this from a dogcart which took my elder sister and myself from the station, while my parents and our Nanny went in the carriage with the luggage.

Although devoted to each other our aunt and uncle were contrasting characters. Aunt Alice was so nervous she refused to travel in any vehicle except a donkey cart at the walk, and as time passed she found even that too alarming. Food and shopping meant as much to her as the Suffolk countryside meant little.

As time passed, Aunt Alice became broader and in the fashion of those days better and more cosily corseted. Movement became increasingly irksome, but little was necessary because an impecunious spinster cousin became her competent unpaid housekeeper and, under the benign direction of Uncle Thorney, really ran the household. In this food was an important element. No question of continental breakfasts at Kelsale! Aunt Alice always appeared in a dressing jacket and with curlers. I and my sister sat each side of her formidable figure and with frequent orders of "eat up, eat up"

The uneven contour of the stopping train which was our joy at the Kelsale level crossing

Putting pennies on the line at the Kelsale level crossing
My sister and I watching excitedly

food would be shovelled on to our plates by her, so as to be certain that we missed nothing.

There was quite a lot to get through. Boiled eggs, scones and toast with jam and marmalade were "constants", never allowed to be missed. But there was also a selection of dishes on the sideboard, for example kidneys, sausages, kedgeree; these too had to be eaten. Then Aunt Alice left us. At about eleven she came down and was brought Bovril and biscuits just to sustain her until lunch. In the afternoon she rested and came down again to a prodigious tea, of which a feature was home baked cakes and honey from the garden hives. No wonder she, and indeed we children too, put on weight.

Uncle Thorney, on the other hand, always managed to remain slim and handsome. He was full of energy, a keen shot, a golfer and interested in everything to do with the countryside. He was forward-looking and it was in character that he bought a Humber motor car as far back as 1906. The car had no hood and no windscreen. The roads then were mostly unsurfaced and when he took us children out for picnics we all arrived white with dust from head to foot. But we loved these expeditions, and the places we saw! Dunwich, Blythburgh, Orford, Sizewell to mention but a few. Then the Aldeburgh golfcourse, where, to my joy, I was let loose to look at birds while he did his round. On our return from Aldeburgh

we always looked out for the postman in case we could give him a lift. In those days the mail arrived on the train at Saxmundham and every day the postman walked the seven miles to deliver it at Aldeburgh and walked back! No wonder he relished a lift.

I was always grateful for a wonderful uncle. He understood and put up with my idiocies better than my father, who was apt to blow up unexpectedly. In fact, Kelsale Place provided all our childish needs and from the first it was a haven of delight.

One of our favourite outings was to walk up to the level crossing beyond the village of Kelsale. There we made a habit of arriving a few minutes before a stopping train to Yarmouth was due. We just had time to put pennies and pins on the railway lines. After the train had passed and the gates were opened again we examined our trophies. If we had been clever the pennies were squashed into the size of five-shilling pieces and the pins into little flat swords. If we had been careless both had been bounced off the line and were probably lost.

But for me, the railway enthusiast, part of the purpose of this escapade was to see the engine of the train and the rolling stock it drew. The train always had the most intriguing and uneven contour. There were old six-wheeler coaches, clerestory semi-corridors, and now and again an up-to-date round-topped corridor coach at the front; and generally the odd horsebox was tacked

67

on the rear.

The engine was always the same type. It was what had been a 2-4-0 with a stovepipe funnel completely converted into an imposing 4-4-0. The old 2-4-0 engines of about 1890, subsequently known as the T.19 class, had done great work in their day. For many years the rebuilds pulled the heaviest trains with equal success. The first batch to be rebuilt about 1902 appeared curiously dumpy, because the 2-4-0 wheel arrangement remained unaltered and above it towered a much larger boiler. In the second batch the single leading axle was replaced by a bogie obtained from old Tank engines which were being broken up. The result was the really handsome 4-4-0 which we always welcomed at our level crossing.

Even if one had to travel on a Sunday, trains always seemed to be punctual then; but our first journey back to London was an exception. To the fury of my father, we were 15 minutes late at Liverpool Street. Probably this was because our train was drawn by an unsuccessful type of engine on what must have been one of its last runs. Two things about this engine I remember well and these give the clue to its type and age: the wheels and the funnel. The funnel was the usual stovepipe, common to many G.E.R. engines, but underneath was a bogie, and this was an exception because other G.E.R. engines had a single axle in front. This engine was one of T.W. Worsdell's, first built as a compound but now converted to simple propulsion. What most caught my eye about this engine was the pair of continuous splashers covering both driving wheels. No other G.E.R. design ever sported that feature as far as I know.

One year my parents decided that

Original 2-4-0 with its Stovepipe chimney.

First batch of rebuilds. Wheels remain as 2-4-0 below a much bigger boiler

Second batch; now 4-4-0 using bogie wheels from old tank engines

At Liverpool Street & its approaches the Teeming
Suburban Life of the G.E.R. seemed to be
dominated by the tiny 0-6-0 Tanks.

One of our last trips from Liverpool Street.
In 1912, the Yarmouth express about to leave,
headed by a "Claud Hamilton" with Belpaire fire box

Leaving the Tiny covered Terminus for Saxmundham.
At Aldeburgh there was always a well kept
2-4-2 Tank in charge.

Sketch map to show the changes since our visits to Saxmundham. (1903 – 1913). Lines now closed are marked with crosses. It will be seen that Yarmouth can now only be reached via Norwich. Saxmundham loses its importance and its excellent train service. The branch line to Aldeburgh has long since been closed, so have many of the other branches running off the old route to Yarmouth

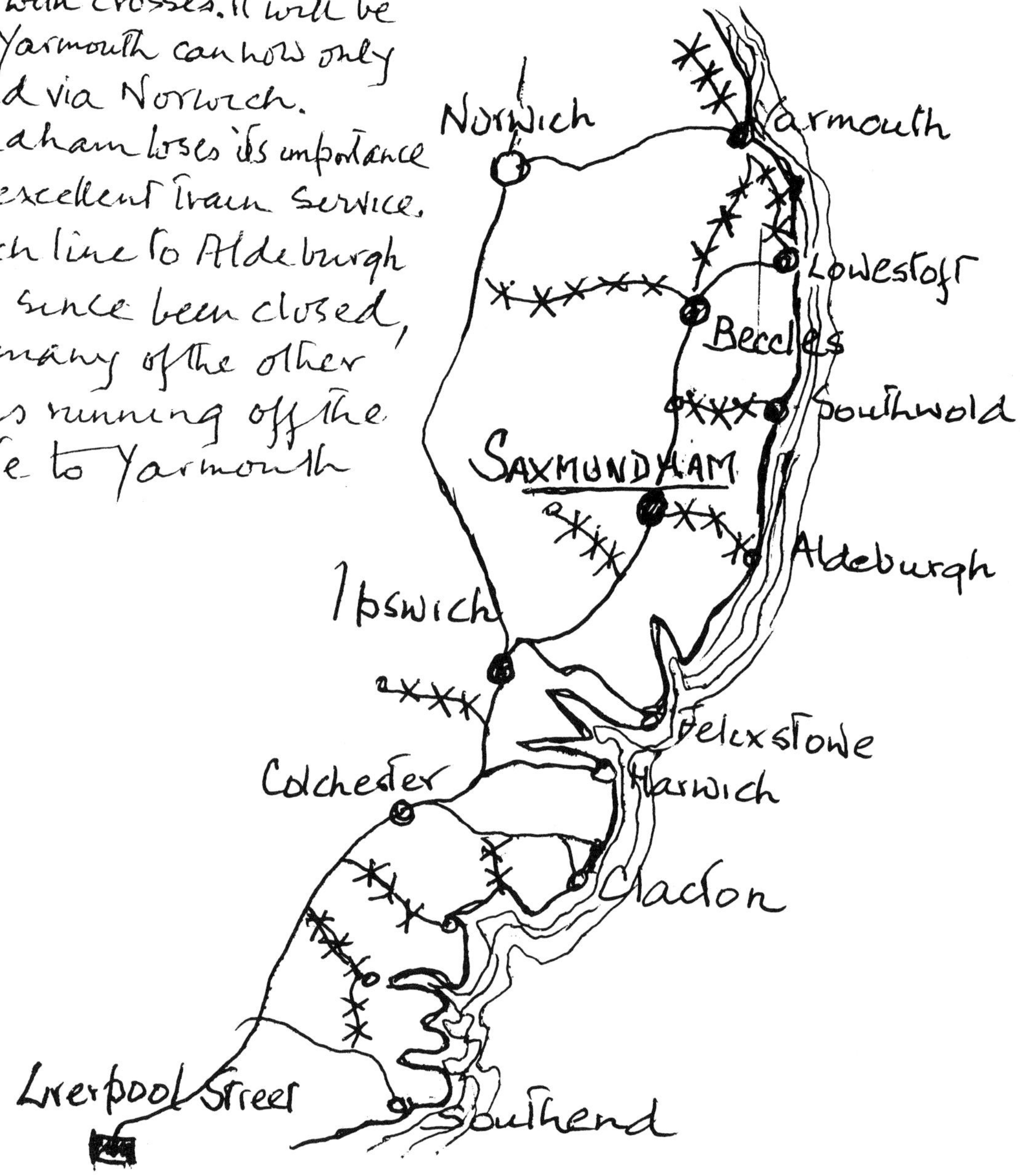

East Anglia

Norwich

Yarmouth

Lowestoft

Beccles

Southwold

SAXMUNDHAM

Aldeburgh

Ipswich

Felixstowe

Colchester

Harwich

Clacton

Liverpool Street

Southend

we should spend our summer holiday at Gorleston, between Yarmouth and Lowestoft, instead of Kelsale. Perhaps they thought we had inflicted ourselves for long enough on my uncle and aunt. We took the Yarmouth express which was the one down train on those days which did not stop at Saxmundham. One of our last views of Kelsale was from the windows of this train. The timings were given to our uncle in advance and he promised to come down to our level crossing to wave to us as we passed through.

Excitement was intense. I and my two sisters were stationed in the corridor well in advance with Nanny. Sure enough as we approached the level crossing at speed there in the distance was Uncle, Aunt and their favourite dog all ready to salute. We passed waving madly with my little sister on tiptoe to get a better view. In the distance as we flashed by we could just make out Kelsale Place and its windmill. My own feelings were mixed; thrill and excitement at the success of our pre-arranged momentary rendezvous but sadness that our destination was not my beloved Kelsale.

The old Worsdell engine which fascinated me, but brought us in 15 minutes late and infuriated my father

Our last view of Kelsale
Place and its Windmill. In
the corridor of the express to
Yarmouth on our way to Gorleston.
My younger sister Ruth on tiptoe
to wave to uncle Thorney as
we passed Kelsale level crossing

CHAPTER EIGHT

FOND

ACQUAINTANCE

Dashing through Dorset. The Race from the West.

WITH THE L.S.W.R.

My parents had been thinking for some time of moving beyond the suburbs, and we spent two years in rooms at Richmond while they looked all round Kent and Surrey for another house. This was a wonderful introduction to the London and South Western Railway of about 1908, with its terminus at Waterloo. There was, of course, the excitement of many new types of engine which I had previously had little opportunity to see. But there was also the prospect of a refreshing change from the rather drab and old-fashioned rolling stock of the S.E.C.R. to the more modern L.S.W.R. carriages with their exotic colouring of pale salmon and deep chocolate, and the chance of seeing dining cars on many of the expresses.

I had a brief experience of the L.S.W.R. a year or two earlier when we went to stay with an aunt at Chiddingfold. Although the journey was intriguing, it was surpassed by the trip from Milford, the nearest station to my aunt's house; we were met by a large trap headed by ponies in tandem with two of our cousins in charge.

This aunt was a widow who had been left to bring up alone a family of one boy and four girls after her husband suddenly died. To us brought up by a strict nanny this family was fascinating. They could not afford such luxuries as nannies and seemed to lead a gloriously free and easy life. They were all older than us; indeed, the boy who was the eldest was already commissioned in the Guides (an elite corps rarely known by its proper name, the Frontier Force Rifles, which served largely in the wilds of Afghanistan and the North West Frontier). He was in India and working for interpreterships in various native languages so that he might be able to augment the meagre family finances.

The two girl cousins aged only about 15 and 17 managed the tandem with skill and confidence and we drew up safely at the house with a flourish. I don't remember ever seeing the ponies or the trap again. I expect the two girls borrowed it for the occasion.

Darling through Richmond. An L.S.W.R 0-4-2 "Jubilee" Class heading the express from Staines as my father and I waited for our train

The Wartime "Solent Special" slipping through
Clapham Junction. Who knew the people in
it? A superheated "Greyhound" in charge.

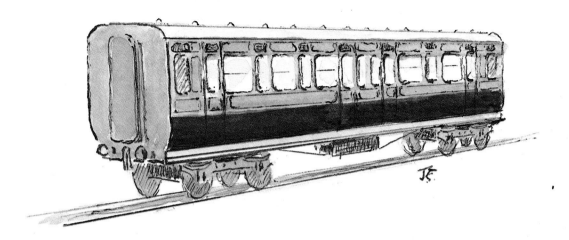

The Salmon and deep chocolate of the LSWR always intrigued me. Here is a typical corridor coach of c.1906, both 1st & 2nd class compartments with sliding doors to the corridors.

The more I saw of the engines of the L.S.W.R. the more they seemed to have a special elegance about them. This was emphasised by some of their nicknames. For example, the Drummond 4-4-0s, first built in 1899 and the mainstay of the company's express trains, were known as the Greyhounds. They were indeed both slinky and speedy and, with minor alterations, had an astoundingly long life full of incident. Greyhounds competed with the G.W.R. Single Drivers in the race from the west heading the Atlantic boat trains between Plymouth and London. For some years the Plymouth boat trains ran in two

parts, the G.W.R. taking the mails, the L.S.W.R. the passengers. It was a later version of the Greyhound hauling the passenger train which crashed at Salisbury when ignoring the speed limit through that station.

The long life of the Greyhound was brought home to me 40-odd years later when travelling home from the War Office one evening from Waterloo to Effingham in Surrey. As we were leaving Clapham Junction a curious train passed us, headed by a superheated and slightly modified Greyhound. The engine was rather ruined by one of R.W. Urie's stovepipe chimneys, and the train

it headed consisted of only two or three Pullman cars. This train turned out to be the special war-time boat train to the Solent which started from Victoria. Waiting on the Solent was the seaplane for neutral Lisbon, then the spy capital of Europe, providing our only gateway to the Continent in the weeks before D-Day. As this curious little train slipped through the Clapham cutting it was intriguing to think what doubtful and perhaps even disguised passengers were sitting back in their Pullman seats hatching their plots.

During this period at Richmond, I often went down to the station to see my

The North London railway. A train on its
way from Richmond to Broad Street
c 1908, headed by the little 4-4-0 Tank
and with small & rather uncomfortable
4 wheeled carriages

By far our commonest
sighting when at Teddington.
A Drummond 0-4-4 Tank,
first built in 1897 and
continued until over too
were working by 1910.

father off on his commuter trip to
London. A few minutes before his train
came in, a fast train from Staines which
was non-stop from Twickenham used
to flash through. Descending the incline
after the bridge over the Thames, it
came through the station at speed.
Sometimes it was headed by the usual
Drummond 0-4-4 Tank, but at others it
had what was to me a rarity, an Adams
0-4-2 Tender engine. At that time,
except for a Drummond chimney, they
were as built in c. 1890.

Another part of Richmond Station
served as the terminus of the old steam
North London Railway line from Broad

Street. Broad Street station is of course
next door to Liverpool Street, so when
we were at Richmond it was not
surprising that we took the North
London on our annual trip to
Saxmundham. It was a curious line with
equally curious little Tank engines and
carriages. The track wandered round the
north of London and in doing so crossed
the main lines out of Paddington, St.
Pancras, Kings Cross and Euston,
providing a fascinating series of vistas
(as it still does today). This journey took
a long time with what seemed to be
stops at every station and my mother
generally became rather restive. The

little four-wheeled carriages, hardly
longer than cattle trucks, were not very
comfortable; but at least we were saved
the trouble of getting across London
from Waterloo.

The little 4-4-0 Tank engines built
way back in 1868 by William Adams
continued to work all passenger trains of
the North London for nearly 60 years.
Except for a change of colour from vivid
green to sombre black they remained
unaltered in all essential parts
throughout their long life. They must
represent something of a record in long
life and efficiency in the locomotive
world.

Our journeys from Richmond to Waterloo gave us a glimpse of the London Brighton & South Coast Railway. Among the multitude of tracks spreading out through Clapham Junction from Waterloo were those of the L.B. & S.C.R. from Victoria. Competition between the Brighton and the L.S.W.R. was such that originally there was no link which would allow a switch of trains from one terminal to the other. Presumably the 1939 war smashed these old-fashioned rivalries and some new points were provided.

The Brighton lines ran parallel with ours after leaving the Junction, then climbed up on a long curved viaduct to cross above the metals of the L.S.W.R.

just before Queens Road Station, Battersea. There was thus quite a long time in which to spot a Brighton train and it was deemed an unlucky day if we drew a blank. Even if no steam-drawn train was seen there was the interest of the Elevated Electric trains which were then something of an innovation. The Brighton Company had first electrified its South London line between Victoria and London Bridge where it had come up against formidable installation problems. The conductor wire and its standards had to be positioned above a track with low bridges, embankments with poor foundations and some curved tunnels. The electric current collector had to be so fashioned that it would be in

continuous contact with the conductor wire at all these varying heights. To meet this problem a special collapsible framework was devised and the end of the carriage roof was flattened in order to provide room to house it.

The flattening of the roof and the curious complex above it produced an odd-looking train bearing little resemblance to any other before or since.

In 1911 this complicated system was extended to Crystal Palace along the Brighton line which ran parallel with the South Western, but it was abandoned when electrification spread to other suburban services. Yet in spite of the initial difficulties in installing the

Jubilee Class 0-4-2

The "Elevated Electric" of the L.B. & S.C.R. climbs
the viaduct after Clapham Junction, bound
for Victoria

The last of Drummond's designs for the L. & S.W.R. Christened the "Paddleboat". A 4 cylinder 4-6-0.

overhead system, time has proved it less vulnerable to snow, frost and accident than the ground conductor rail system which for many years replaced it.

After nearly two years' searching, my parents were evidently disillusioned by their failure to find any house they liked beyond the suburbs. To the disgust of us children they settled for one at Teddington only a few miles away. We were disappointed because we had hoped for a more rural locality, but apart from nearby Bushey Park, then comparatively wild and

unfrequented, Teddington was suburban. The railway station was at the furthest point of a loop line from Waterloo which went out via Richmond and Twickenham and back via Kingston to join the main line at Malden. This provided a frequent service to Teddington in either direction, but most trains stopped at every station and it was therefore a slow and tedious journey.

There was however one fast train in the morning which ran non-stop after Norbiton. My father generally took this train which left about 8.35 a.m. and

during my school holidays I often walked down to the station to see him off. I became quite pally with the driver and we used to wave to each other. It was curious that this one fast train was headed by what was almost a vintage engine – a 4-4-2 Tank built by Adams before 1890. It had outside cylinders and in all essentials was original. I thought it attractive. According to my father this train was always punctual in spite of a tight schedule – 35 minutes instead of the 53 minutes of others.

C. 1910
The 8.35 leaves Teddington
Adams 4-4-2 Tank.
I wave to the friendly driver

J.F.

CHAPTER NINE

FENCHURCH STREET AND THE "SOUTHEND"

My father's office was in Billiter Street (since entirely rebuilt) not far from Fenchurch Street Station. His works were in the dockland of North Greenwich. When we were at Blackheath he used to take the train from Lewisham to Cannon Street if going to his office. If he first wanted to go to the works he would take the Greenwich foot tunnel under the Thames which landed him close to North Greenwich. Often I and my elder sister walked with him to the entrance of the Greenwich tunnel, but occasionally I was taken up with my mother to meet him at his office.

One such day, probably about 1906, I was introduced to Fenchurch Street. It was the terminus of the London Tilbury and Southend Railway. I had already seen the termini of other systems in the metropolis with their imposing approaches and vast interiors, but Fenchurch Street bore little likeness to them. Among a maze of city streets one turned a corner, and there was the entrance to the station, far from imposing and with surprisingly little turn-round room even for the horse-drawn transport of that era. Nor was the interior much more impressive. In all it seemed to me more like a glorified

suburban station.

But then I did not know anything about the L.T. & S.R. In fact the "Southend" as it was generally called was unlike any system running into London with the possible exception of the North London Railway. It was originally confined to one route to the towns of its name, with intermediate stations; then extended another three and a half miles to Shoeburyness. At Barking it met up with the Metropolitan District. This junction was used to run through trains from Charing Cross on the District Railway to Southend and Shoebury. One train was a Saturday

The "Saturday Night only" at Charing Cross

night special laid on so that revellers in the West End could return to Essex without the risky business of finding a cab to take them to Fenchurch Street.

By 1917 the strength of the armed forces in places served by the L. T. & S. R., such as Tilbury and Shoeburyness, had been much increased. A number of young Gunner officers were sent to Shoeburyness to await posting, among them myself and several who had been my contemporaries at the Royal Military Academy, Woolwich. We were all nearing our nineteenth birthdays and at that age eligible for war service.

Not unnaturally perhaps we sought the lights of London during these last days before being plunged into the bloodbath of the Western Front. On Saturday we had our only chance. We could then reach the West End in time for dinner or a theatre followed by a snack. At about midnight, we stumbled into our seats on the Saturday night special at Charing Cross Underground station, gratefully if perhaps a little unsteadily.

This train was an unusually thoughtful provision for servicemen at play, many for the last time. It also had unusual features. It was I imagine the only corridor train regularly to run on this line because the L. T. & S. R. used no corridor stock on its short length. Where the carriages for this Saturday night special came from I never discovered. When I travelled on this train from Charing Cross in February 1917 we had an electric District engine up to Barking, then the steam L. T. & S. R. engine to take us on to Southend and Shoeburyness.

Although the L. T. & S. R. had a comparatively short life (it was taken over by the Midland in 1912) it was possibly unique in operating its passenger trains with nothing but Tank engines throughout its existence. The most successful of these were built by Sharp Stewart & Co. about 1896; and there were several subsequent editions with larger boilers and the same 4-4-2 wheel arrangement. When I first went to Fenchurch Street these engines reigned supreme. Even some 20 years later they were still the mainstay of the Southend.

The first of a long line of 4-4-2 Tanks built by Sharp Stewart for the "Southend"

The last of the long line of 4-4-2s for the "Southend" T. Whitelegg's handsome design

Slipping down to Tilbury docks.

CHAPTER TEN

TO CHELTENHAM BY SLIP CARRIAGE

When I went away to school in Cheltenham at the age of thirteen I had the novel experience of being "slipped" from an express train. The prospect of school was frightening, but fortunately there was the interest of the train journey to calm my nerves. We started from Paddington and I was in love both with that station and the Great Western Railway. I had heard something of "slip carriages", of which the G.W.R. had many, but had never seen them, let alone travelled in one. The advantages were obvious. Instead of the time-losing business of stopping, disconnecting carriages for a through connection from the express and starting again from a dead stop, there was merely a sharp slow down and subsequent acceleration. Equally obvious was the care needed in such an exact operation. There was also the special equipment required to free the couplings of the carriage to be slipped while still in motion. In fact the slip carriage had to be specially built and extra training provided for the man to operate it.

The train was a Worcester express non-stop to Evesham. There was one slip carriage only and of course in order to be slipped it had to be the last carriage of the train. This one carriage had to carry passengers for a number of branch line stations, of which the last was Cheltenham; inevitably the compartments were packed. That didn't worry me then, in fact it was rather cheering in my depressed state. I was agog to find out how everything was organized.

I knew we were to be slipped at

Marshalling duty at Paddington. A 2-4-0 Tank in original condition with condenser pipes c. 1908

Kingham; so to other passengers' disgust and discomfort, I insisted on struggling to the window as we approached the station. The brakes of our carriage were put on very hard; and the rest of the train accelerated briskly. Then after this initial braking our carriage continued slowly and gently into Kingham Station while the express rocketed away into the distance.

We came to rest and our carriage was joined to a short train headed by an old 2-4-0 Tank. The subsequent journey was a rarity. We crossed the main grain of the Cotswolds, sweating and puffing up the hills and dashing down the valleys; and the names of the stations after leaving Kingham! Stow-on-the-Wold, Bourton-on-the-Water, Notgrove, Andoversford, Charlton Kings, Cheltenham. This branch was all a single line, now dead unfortunately. My head was continually at the window.

On the slip journeys of those days generally one carriage was slipped, but there were some exceptions. The G.E.R. had some slips of more than one carriage, each dropped off at different places; and rarely another carriage was added to the slip so that two were dropped off at the same time – a manoeuvre which must have required very careful handling. The G.W.R. ran one slip to an important main line station – Bath. I discovered this as an avid reader of the *Railway Magazine* of those days. It showed a list of the fastest runs of over 100 miles (in 1909 I think), and the winner was a "slip" at Bath.

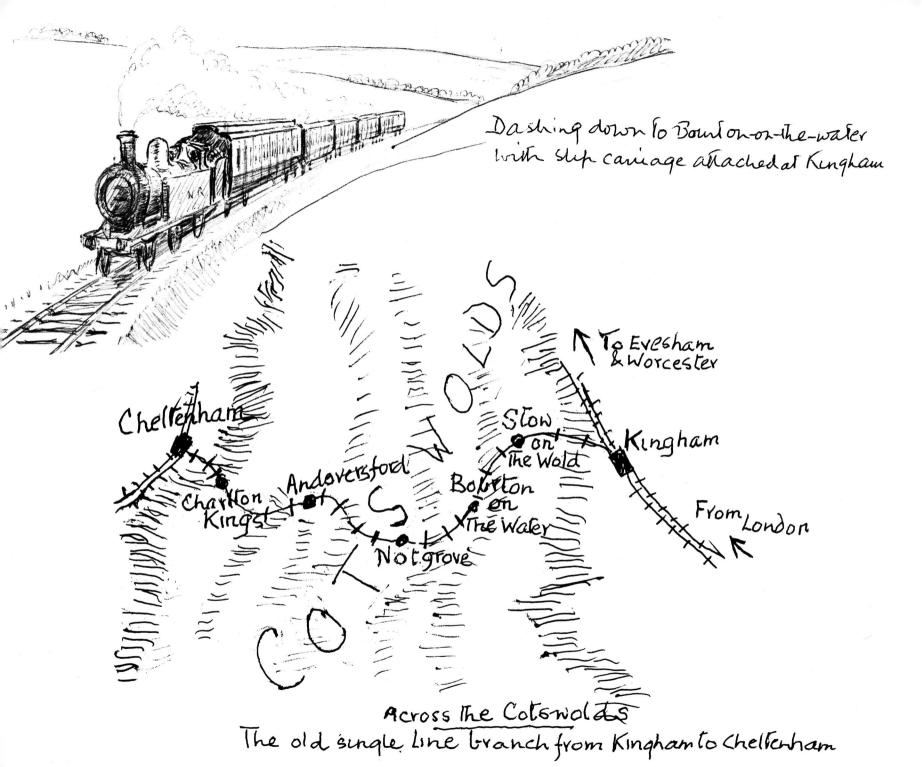

Dashing down to Bourton-on-the-water
with slip carriage attached at Kingham

To Evesham & Worcester

Kingham

From London

COTSWOLDS

Cheltenham

Charlton Kings

Andoversford

Notgrove

Bourton on The Water

Stow on The Wold

Across the Cotswolds
The old single line branch from Kingham to Cheltenham

Our "slip" at Kingham

CHAPTER ELEVEN

FROM RUGELEY BY L.N.W.R.

At the end of the summer term at Cheltenham in 1912, I attended an Officers' Training Corps Camp on Cannock Chase. When the camp broke up a special was arranged by the London & North Western Railway to take us from the nearest station, Rugeley, to Euston. Our carriages were the typical rather dull flat-roof specimens which the L.N.W.R. had used throughout their system for many years. But heading our special we had an Experiment; in spite of having driving wheels only 6ft. 3in. in diameter these six-coupled engines were fast and our special reached Euston four minutes early.

On the journey there should have been much to see but my luck was not in. The L.N.W.R. enjoyed a vast goods traffic of all sorts of which the movement of coal formed an important part. I was therefore on the look-out for what was then a fairly new mineral engine, a large 0-8-0. But nothing more modern was to be seen than the 0-6-0s built many years earlier. In fact Webb first built this class of engine in 1873 with the coal trade in mind. They proved so simple to produce and so satisfactory in their work that they were made without alteration for the next 20 years. By that time their numbers had risen to 500, so no wonder I saw no other type.

Then there was just a chance that

the Chief Engineer's inspection carriage might show itself. Several railway systems had made up special carriages for their chief engineers or directors. Both the Midland and L.N.W.R. had used their old Single Drivers as motive power for these carriages, and the latter which I hoped to see was particularly unusual. It was made up into one single entity. But that was not all; the engine part was the famous *Cornwall* with driving wheels of 8ft. 6in., which had been withdrawn from service a few years previously after completing nearly one million miles.

By the time we reached Euston my appearance was thoroughly revolting. Still in my scruffy corps uniform I was unwashed, dishevelled and hatless because my "cheesecutter" corps cap had disappeared on the journey as I craned from the window in vain hopes of a spectacular sighting.

The L.N.W.R. managed to get themselves known as the Premier Line. I used to think this something of a misnomer. Certainly they went in for advertisement and produced more postcards of their engines than any other line; my collection abounded in them. But their engines were black which was dull, although picked out in red, and their carriages looked old-fashioned outwardly compared with those of the other lines to the north and inside were none too comfortable.

Our Special from Rugeley headed
by an "Experiment" 4-6-0

A 'Jumbo' at speed

"Hardwicke", hero of the 1895 Race to the North,
flashing through a Station on the way to Carlisle

The railway's main line out of Euston began with a series of smoky tunnels and then passed through a flat and rather uninteresting stretch of countryside. Probably it was the magnificently designed track from Euston as far as Crewe which gained them their reputation. Compared with most other systems, this was a smooth race track and gave the west coast route to Scotland an initial advantage over the east coast route.

My father had told me about the competition between the two routes to Edinburgh from London, leading to the famous Races to the North. Many years later I was fascinated to hear from an old lady (the late Lady Dunphie) that as a teenager she had travelled on the record-breaking train pulled by *Hardwicke* in 1895. From Wales she had joined it at Crewe for Scotland. The record-breaking performance took place oddly enough not on the London-Crewe but on the hillier Crewe-Carlisle section of the line. She and her parents had been literally hurled into the train at Crewe and its lurching and bumping on its journey north had made her physically sick. As the train sped down at tremendous speed from Shap summit towards Carlisle, her mother too was nearly defeated; clinging to the arm of the carriage she went white with fear.

I have tried to picture *Hardwicke* as she might have looked on this famous trip, flashing through a station after leaving Crewe and building up speed for the ascent of Shap.

Many years later, during the period leading up to the Second World War, competition between the east and west coast routes to Scotland revived, this time between the two great amalgamated systems, the London and North Eastern Railway and the London Midland Scottish. The best efforts of the former I experienced on several occasions. From Catterick camp where I was based in 1937 I used to join a Scotch Express from Edinburgh when it stopped at Darlington for London. In 1938 I took this flyer again in the opposite direction from London for its stop at York which was then my destination. Behind the Gresley Pacifics, both journeys were terrific, yet naturally my mind turned back 30-odd years with some nostalgia.

L.N.W.R.
A standard 0-6-0
goods engine heading a coal train

the "Cornwall" built onto the inspection
saloon of the Chief Mechanical Engineer of L.N.W.R

One of Ramsbottom's tiny 7'6" singles.
They first appeared as early as 1859,
and with a cab in place of the original
windscreen they ran for nearly half a century.

CHAPTER TWELVE

TALES OF THE HIGHLANDS

My parents were lifelong friends of a couple who frequently appeared at our house at Blackheath. They were alleged to be restless and certainly they always seemed to be moving from one house to another. But they must have been richer than we were, because for year after year they rented a shooting lodge in the Highlands for the grouse season. My father was a keen shot and I can just, but only just, remember my mother's excitement when telling me that they had been invited to join these friends at the lodge they had taken near Blair Athol. It must have been as long ago as 1904 yet what is still quite clear is my father's description of the train journey there and back.

They travelled to Blair Athol by the night sleeper from Euston, later to be called the *Royal Highlander*, and came back by day. First, there was the fascinating description of how they boarded the train at about 8 o'clock and got settled in their sleeper, followed by the arrival of the sleeping car attendant for their orders for calling with, of course, early morning tea. But the details of the railways on the west coast route to the Highlands via Carlisle and Perth, more vivid on the return journey by day, were even better. I was just beginning to learn something about the L.N.W.R. from a kind elderly cousin at Crewe, but the railways of Scotland were new ground. Now two of them were vividly described, although it was many years before I could transform these old descriptions into first-hand experience.

At Carlisle, in the early hours, the

The Euston sleeper from Inverness climbing to Slochd Muir summit.
c1905, headed by Highland Railway's "Castle" class 4-6-0

sombre black of the L.N.W.R. engine was replaced by the blue and shining Caledonian Railway locomotive. They reached Perth at about 6.30 in the morning. Here the Highland Railway took over from the Caledonian. Green engines were substituted for the blue. Then the long climb to Blair Athol. This alone was a marvellous tale for the ears of a very small boy. Two engines headed the train and both were Six Couplers, presumably the Castle class, which were then the Highland's latest express engines. Blair Athol is almost two-thirds of the way up to the summit of Druimuachdar 1,484 ft. above sea level, the highest point reached by any main-line railway in the British Isles.

All this I was told and how it was a single line which soon after leaving Perth wound through magnificent country. There were the lush and wooded valleys of the Tummel and Garry and the famous pass of Killiecrankie before the wilder uplands of the grouse moors were reached. Another thing my father told me concerned the danger of drifting snow in these high open moorland reaches of the railway. To guard against this, lines of fencing made of up-ended sleepers were built at various points on either side of the line. Many years later I observed these with interest; there seemed to be no system in their placing. But the areas where drifting snow may settle are difficult to assess and no doubt years of practical experience enabled the engineers to decide where the risk to the track was greatest and where protection should be given. Nothing can guard with absolute certainty against the vagaries of snow and wind on these great open heights. Even today nature sometimes defeats us. Only a few winters ago a train on what used to be the Highland Railway was snow-bound for nearly 24 hours.

A "Jones goods" tops the
Summit at Druimuach-dar
and passes a snow-screen fence

Early morning. The "night sleeper"
leaves Perth in charge of two
"Castle Class' Highland 4-6-0s, both
coaling up for the great climb.

All the earlier engines of the Highlands, up to the famous Jones Goods, had curious louvres on their funnels which are visible in the sketch of that engine. As far as I know they were not adopted by any other railway company. These louvres were possibly designed to increase the exhaust draught when the engines were running at speed, though no one knows for certain. But they must have had some useful purpose for a first-class locomotive engineer to install them, and there is no doubt about the class of Mr. Jones or the success of his engines.

My father told me of the famous C.R. Single driver tearing past in the 1888 Race to the North. Might it have looked like this?

Over the Hump. Speeding south after Shap, the day
express from Scotland headed by LNWR "Precursor".

CHAPTER THIRTEEN

A FAREWELL ON THE M. & S.W.J.

King Edward VII had been dead for some years when I made a memorable journey to and from the West Country. It was memorable not so much for its railway significance, though that existed in good measure, but because it came at the end of an era, just days before the great change of life represented by the First World War. The date was August 1914.

Unlike today, when the media plug all that is disturbing in world affairs, we were blissfully ignorant of every approaching crisis. The summer term at Cheltenham College ended and I went to camp as usual with the O.T.C., this time to Tidworth Pennings on Salisbury Plain. The journey from Cheltenham to Ludgershall, the station for our camp, absorbed all my attention. Our train

wandered over the Cotswolds to Cirencester, through Marlborough and the Savernake Forest. It was mostly a single line with fine scenery throughout. Even as a young schoolboy I enjoyed all this, but it was only later that I realised the significance of the route we were taking. It was in fact the Midland & South Western Junction Railway; a company whose story highlights the

Our "special from Cheltenham had the honour of being drawn by one of the engines built specially for the Midland and South Western. It was a chunky little 2-4-0 and is pictured arriving at Ludgershall. Just a platform & siding with Salisbury Plain as background.

JE.

changes in travel so noticeable since the early 1900s. Heading our train was one of the few engines – not more than about 30 in all – that the Junction Railway owned, a chunky little 2-4-0. I was glad to have had this rare glimpse of railway history.

In mid-Victorian days when Southampton began its impressive development as a port the idea of a direct link with the industrial Midlands was discussed. Even as far back as 1845, during the period of railway expansion mania, such a line had been proposed and Robert Stephenson was engaged to build it, but the project came to nothing. Years later a number of piecemeal efforts were made to establish such a link and these initiatives were ultimately brought to fruition by the formation of the Midland & South Western Junction company in 1884.

London & South Western Railway

Waterloo "A" Signal box c 1908. On the right is a "Greyhound" preparing to take charge of a Bournemouth express

106

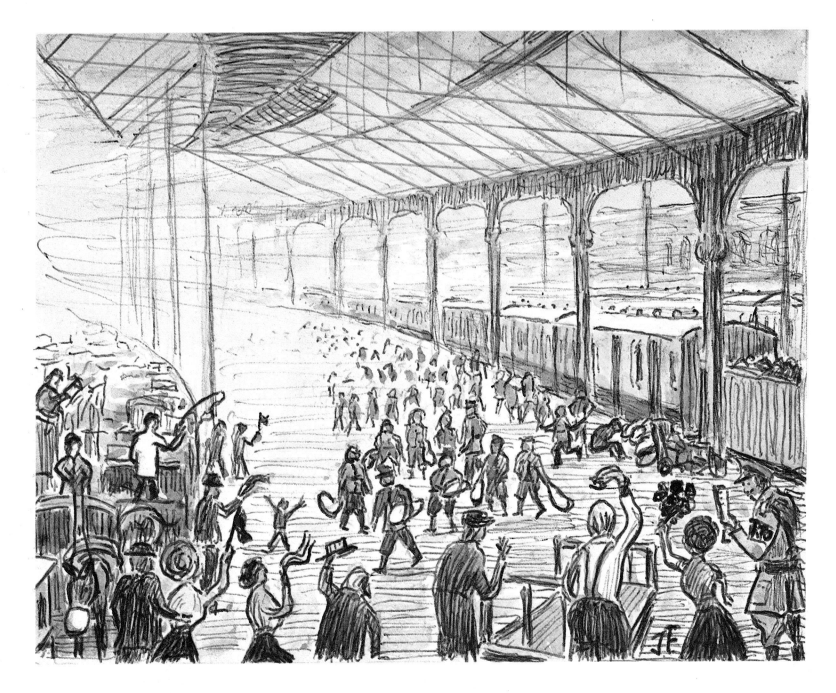

August 1914.
We were astonished at our greeting at Waterloo

The route was to be a mixture of existing track owned by other companies and specially constructed new stretches. One part that had to be built was from Andoversford (on the G.W.R.) to Andover (L.S.W.R.) and it was all to be single track. By running over the existing G.W.R. metals from Cheltenham to Andoversford and over the L.S.W.R. in the later stages to Southampton the complete link was opened in 1891.

After a tricky start the company kept out of bankruptcy for a decade or so. Indeed a number of through carriages from Southampton were arranged to Birmingham, the West Riding towns of Yorkshire and even to Sheffield, and during the First World War it provided the nation with a valuable service getting troops and supplies to Southampton. But the disadvantages of the new heavily graded single line together with the opening of an easier route via Newbury soon took toll of the profits. Eventually the line was taken over by the G.W.R.

Some years ago the vital stretch from Andoversford to Andover, which took so long to build, was abandoned. So died the M. & S.W.J. Railway. Seemingly so important, and indeed proving adequate in the conditions of the 19th century, it became redundant in the conditions of the 20th.

The first six days of camp passed in the normal Army fashion. My most vivid memory concerned the washing-up arrangements. Our tent of eight nasty little bodies was issued with just two washing-up cloths to last us for the whole 10 days we were to be there. As we seemed to live on an exclusive diet of mutton stew the state of these two small cloths can be imagined. Certainly none of us was fastidious, but for myself and I think for the other seven this was not a pleasant memory. Someone should have told us how to wash the cloths!

On the sixth night of our camp we were told our country was at war, that we would therefore break up and entrain at Ludgershall Station by 6.30 a.m. next morning. We duly humped our bulging kitbags and ourselves down to the station – some three miles away – as dawn was breaking. Our train left punctually at 6.30 a.m., headed by an L.S.W.R. mixed traffic 4-4-0, the usual standby for Army specials.

On our arrival at Waterloo the scene was staggering. Here were we, a dirty, scruffy collection of youngsters, hungry and dishevelled in our hastily donned O.T.C. uniforms. Yet we were greeted and applauded and embraced as little heroes. As mobilisation movements of the British Expeditionary Force had just begun I can only think that we were regarded as the advance guard – undoubtedly one of the youngest and worst dressed ever!

The Race from The West

1905. Dashing through Dorset. LSW.R
A "Greyhound" in the Ocean Mail
races which led to the Salisbury
disaster of 1906.

INDEX